WATER Animals

Seals, Squids, Fish, & More!

Carus Publishing Company
Peterborough, NH
www.cricketmag.com

Staff
Editorial Director: Lou Waryncia
Project Editor: Charles Baker III
Designer: Brenda Ellis, Graphic Sense
Proofreader: Eileen Terrill

Text Credits
The content of this volume is derived from articles that first appeared in *CLICK*® and *ASK*®
magazines. Contributors: Buffy Silverman ("Sea Star"), Meg Moss ("Is This a Giant Squid?"),
Charnan Simon ("A Pond for Maddie"), Kathleen Weidner Zoehfeld ("Home From the Sea" and
"Pond Builders").

Picture Credits
Photos.com: 4, 5, 16, 24, 28; Elsa Warnick: 6–9; Smithsonian Institution: 10, 11, 13–15;
Marcy Ramsey: 18–21; Diane Blasius: 22–27.

Cover
Picture Quest.

The Library of Congress Cataloging-in-Publication Data for *Water Animals* is available at
http://catalog.loc.gov.

Carus Publishing
30 Grove Street, Peterborough, NH 03458
www.cricketmag.com

Printed in China

Table of Contents

Breathing Underwater

Breathe in. AH! It feels good when the air fills your lungs inside your chest. Breathing is how you get oxygen, a part of the air that your body needs to live.

Animals that live in the ocean need oxygen, too. Whales and dolphins are mammals that come to the surface to breathe. They have lungs like you do, but they breathe through a blowhole on top of their heads. When they dive underwater, they hold their breath. They can stay under a long time. When they come back to the surface, they breathe out a big gust of air through their blowholes.

Fish don't have lungs. How do they breathe? How do they get oxygen? Instead of lungs, fish have gills. A fish breathes by opening and closing its mouth. When it opens its mouth, it lets water in. When it closes its mouth, it pushes the water over its gills.

There's oxygen in water, just as there's oxygen in the air. The gills take in the oxygen when the water flows over them. That way the fish can live and breathe underwater.

Some big, active fish, such as a bluefin tuna, need lots of oxygen. They swim with their mouths open so more water flows over their gills.

Sometimes when you need lots of oxygen, such as when you run or play hard, you breathe with your mouth open, too.

Home From the Sea

In late November, the beaches of California's Ano Nuevo Island start getting crowded. But these quiet beaches, and others like them, are not packed with sunbathers. They are crowded with huge, clumsy blobs of blubber, the thick layer of fat under their skin, that crawl across the sand like caterpillars the size of hippos.

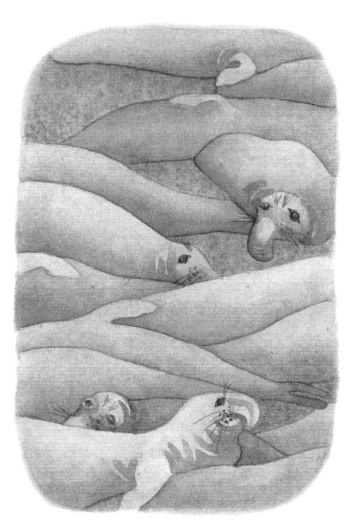

These furry blobs are male elephant seals. Their floppy trunklike noses give you one clue about how elephant seals got their name. The other clue is their size. The biggest males can weigh as much as 5,000 pounds — more than a minivan! Every winter they return home to California from their favorite fishing spots near the Aleutian Islands in western Alaska, 3,000 miles away.

They look funny on land, as they drag themselves along on their bellies, but they are fast, graceful swimmers. And they can dive deeper than any other type of seal. Some go down almost a mile to get their favorite foods. Their blubber helps their bodies withstand the bitter cold and high pressure of the deep, deep sea.

Just like people, seals need to breathe air. But elephant seals can hold their breath underwater for over an hour! They can even sleep underwater! While at sea, they dive almost nonstop. For months, the seals dive and eat fish after fish, growing as big and as fat as they can.

Now the male seals have come home to California to fight. They throw back their heads and roar. They bite and push each other around, protected by the thick skin around their necks and chests. Only the biggest and strongest males will get to mate with the females.

Female elephant seals don't have big, long noses. And they are much lighter than the males. Even the biggest females weigh only about 1,600 pounds. While the males were swimming north along the coast for fish, the females swam west, far out into the Pacific Ocean. They zigzagged from place to place in search of a lighter diet of squid. But they, too, return home to breed.

When they arrive at the beach in December, the females gather together in groups. Within a few days, each female gives birth to a little pup. For four weeks, the pups drink their mothers' rich milk. They grow fast, gaining up to 10 pounds a day.

Once the pups are big and fat, the adult seals mate and then go back to the sea. Elephant seals do not eat when they are on land. So, all of them are very hungry and eager to begin the long journey back to their favorite feeding areas.

The pups, now called weaners, stay on shore for two or three more months. They play and paddle around in the water, slowly learning how to swim. Soon they will leave the quiet beaches and begin their first long migration in search of food.

Is This a Giant Squid?

No, it isn't. No one has ever seen or photographed a giant squid in its natural habitat. And it's driving scientists crazy!

Then how do we know they exist? Over the years, more than 250 dead or dying giant squid have washed ashore. Others get caught in fishing nets. Some leave sucker marks on huge whales, and sometimes, bits and pieces of giant squid turn up in a whale's stomach. Scientists can learn some things from these clues and from smaller species of squid that they've studied. Even so, the habits and behavior of this deep-sea giant remain a mystery.

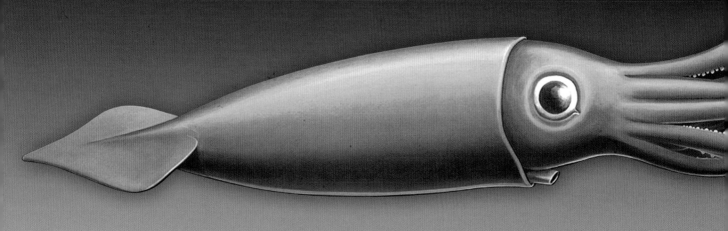

Giant squid might be quite smart, since they have well-developed brains. Perhaps they're even smart enough to outsmart the scientists looking for them. Could it be that we've never seen a live giant squid because they don't want to be found?

Battle of the Heavyweights

Only one other animal in the ocean is big enough to tangle with the giant squid — the 50-ton sperm whale. And tangle they do. Whales feed on all kinds of squid, but dinnertime gets exciting when giants are on the menu. Some people claim to have seen

Did you know?
The eyes of the giant squid are the largest in the animal kingdom. They are the size of soccer balls. And, they help it see in the deep ocean, where there is no sunlight.

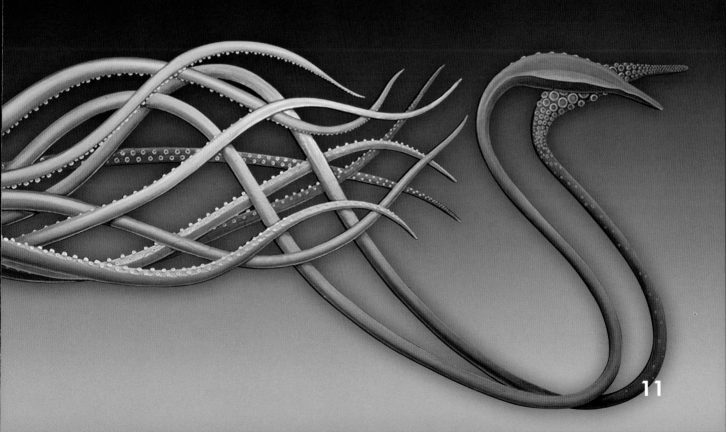

whales battling giant squid on the ocean surface, but the fight usually goes on underwater. Though sperm whales must surface to breathe (because they are mammals), they can dive very deep in their hunt for giant squid. They can stay down for 90 minutes. The stomachs of dead whales often contain bone-like beaks of giant squid, some six inches long, which the whales can't digest. And on the whales' skin can be seen circular marks made by the squid's toothed suckers during the struggle. The whale usually wins.

A Spineless Wonder

A scientist from Denmark decided that these mysterious beasts were a type of giant squid. He named them *Architeuthis* ("Archie" to its friends), which means "first squid."

Naming the creature gave it an identity but did not solve the mysteries surrounding it. How big can it get? In which oceans does it live? How deep can it dive? How fast does it move? How does it hunt? How many are there? Still, in the past 200 years, scientists have learned a few things about Archie.

Squids have no backbones or other bones,

Did you know?
In ancient times, sailors from Norway told tales of the *kraken,* a terrifying creature with many arms that attacked ships.

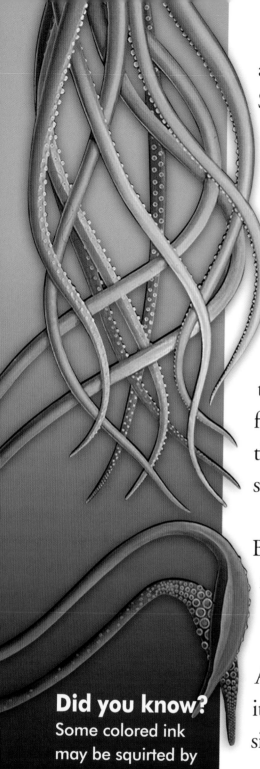

and they are covered with rubbery flesh. Scientists believe the giant squid may grow to 60 feet long, twice the length of a bus, and weigh approximately a ton (about 2,000 pounds). Its eight long, thick arms are lined with barbed suckers. Two even longer tentacles can reach out and clamp down on prey, which the squid then draws into its mouth. Its large, parrotlike (yes, as in the bird!) beak is buried deep in muscle. Inside this powerful beak, toothlike ridges shred food for the squid to swallow. (Food must pass through the squid's brain to reach its stomach, so the pieces can't be too big!)

The giant squid moves by "jet propulsion." Beneath its head, a short "hose" extends and rotates. Through this, the animal blasts water to push itself backward or forward. Scientists disagree about how fast the squid can move. A lighter-than-water fluid in its tissues gives it "neutral buoyancy." This means it can drift silently in the dark water, ready to ambush prey.

While many squid squirt ink to confuse predators, the giant squid has only a small ink sac. However, scientists believe that it can hide itself in some amazing ways. Special cells in

Did you know?
Some colored ink may be squirted by squid to impress that "certain other" squid during the mating process.

its skin allow it to change color from silver to brown to purplish to red. Some colors may allow the squid to sneak up on prey.

Squid Squads

Because giant squid have been stranded on beaches around the world, we think they live in every ocean and probably live in underwater canyons, where food is plentiful. Using undersea robots and manned research subs, scientists plunge as far down as they can, hoping to observe the camera-shy squid "at home." Clyde Roper, a well-known scientist who studies squids, once led an expedition to attach "crittercams" to the heads of huge sperm whales. These whales often enjoy a dinner of tasty squid, and Clyde hoped to get a whale's-eye view of the hunt. He had no such luck. Steve O'Shea, another leading squid expert, started small. He hoped to raise a giant squid in captivity and ventured out night after night to capture baby giants feeding just below the surface of the water. Although he nabbed a batch of babies, each one died within days. This happened because O'Shea did not know the right food, light, and water pressure to keep the babies alive.

Pond Builders

In the summer, two of young beavers wander up and down a forest stream, looking for the perfect place to make their home. Twigs, bark, and leaves are the beavers' favorite foods. So, they choose a stretch of creek with lots of trees growing nearby.

The trees are important for another reason, too. In the fall, the beavers cut down trees and use them to build a sturdy dam across the creek. Soon there will be a deep, wide pond!

Beavers are slow and clumsy on land, but they are great swimmers. When they make their pond, they will be able to swim away from enemies — such as bears, wolves, and mountain lions — that can easily catch them on land. With its four chisel-like front teeth, a beaver can cut down a small tree in minutes. Once a tree is down, the beavers gnaw off branches and haul them to the stream. They lay mud and rocks on them to hold them in place. Water begins to collect behind their wall of branches, and a pond has begun to form!

Wherever the beavers hear the sound of water running through their new dam, they rush to plug up the spaces with grass, roots, and mud.

Little by little, the beavers add more branches and more mud. As the dam gets bigger and more solid, the pond grows wider and deeper. Now, it's time for the beavers to build their home, or lodge.

They make a big pile of rocks, mud, and branches in the middle of the pond. Then they tunnel in from underwater and gnaw out a hollow chamber, which has a lower level for eating and a nice, dry upper level for sleeping. Here, the beavers stay warm and cozy through the winter.

In the spring, their babies are born. Bears and wolves may spot the youngsters from shore. But the wide water of their pond and the sturdy walls of their lodge help keep the beavers safe and sound.

Sea Star

Sea Star grips the rocky ocean bottom near shore. Waves crash over her, but she holds on tight. Tiny suckers underneath her five arms keep her in place. The suckers are on the tips of hundreds of little tubes that Sea Star uses as feet to crawl along the ocean floor.

The ocean waves carry the smell of clams to her. Sea Star is always ready for a meal. Her muscles pull water inside her body. Her tube feet fill like little balloons, and their suckers grab onto the sea floor. Then Sea Star squeezes the water out of some of her tube

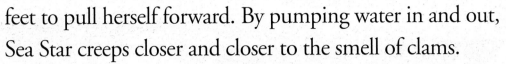

feet to pull herself forward. By pumping water in and out, Sea Star creeps closer and closer to the smell of clams.

When Sea Star reaches her goal, she climbs on top of a clam. The clam snaps its two shells closed, hiding its soft body. Clamping on with her tube feet, Sea Star tries to pry the shells open. She pulls and pulls, but the clam's strong muscles hold tight. Finally, Sea Star budges the shells apart.

Sea Star flips her stomach out through the mouth on her underside and into the tiny gap between the shells. She squirts chemicals that soften the clam's body. When the clam turns soupy, she swallows her meal. All that remains are two empty shells.

After finishing her meal, Sea Star clings to a rock in the shallow water and rests. Tiny baby animals called barnacles drift in the water that flows over her. Some try to attach onto Sea Star's back. But Sea Star has little pinchers on her spiny skin. The pinchers snap at the barnacles, chasing them away. It is important for Sea Star to keep her skin clean. She takes in oxygen through her bumpy skin and cannot get enough if barnacles grow there.

A gull lands near Sea Star and spies her beneath the water. The gull plunges its head underwater and grabs onto one of Sea Star's arms. It holds Sea Star in its beak. Before the bird can swallow, two other gulls fly at it. Sea Star slips out of the gull's beak as the bird takes flight.

The gull broke off one of Sea Star's arms. But Sea Star is not bothered. She creeps into a crack between two rocks on her remaining four arms.

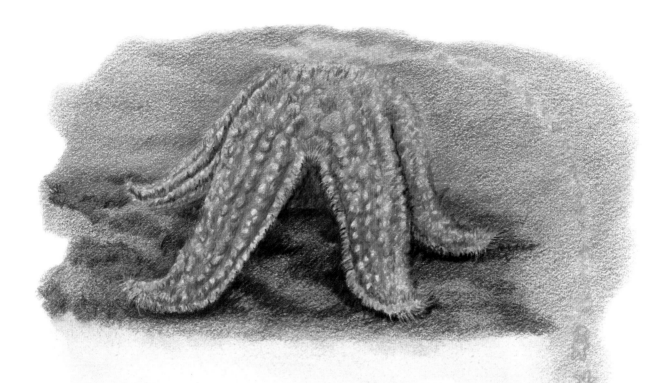

That spring, Sea Star's missing arm grows back. At first, it is tiny. Slowly, it grows larger and larger. After several months, Sea Star's new arm is as long as the others.

Sea Star has also been growing eggs inside her body. Now thousands of them stream out of openings on her arms and into the water. When an egg is fertilized by a male sea star, it begins to grow. Soon, hundreds and hundreds of baby sea stars, called larvae, float in the water.

The sea star larvae look nothing like Sea Star. Fish and other sea animals will eat most of them. Others will be washed ashore by the ocean waves. Only a few will survive and grow to look like Sea Star. Someday, those sea stars will crawl on their tube feet along the rocky bottom near the shore, hunting for a seafood meal.

A Pond for Maddie

Maddie liked everything about her new house except the stinky back garden. "Yuck," she said, holding her nose. "This place needs some air freshener."

Maddie's dad sniffed. "It's a little strong," he admitted. "Let's see what we've got." He waded into the overgrown bushes and kicked aside a pile of dead leaves.

"It's an artificial pond!" he called out.

Maddie came closer. There was just a big hole in the ground, filled with a little water and a lot of dead, slimy leaves. Stinky!

"Oh! I'm not looking forward to digging this out," Mom said.

"Dig it out?" said Dad. "Let's bring it back to life!"

Bringing a pond back to life was hard work. First they pumped out the old, dirty water. Then they tackled the muck.

"Why can't we just use rakes and shovels?" Maddie asked. Even with big, thick gardening gloves, she didn't want to touch anything.

Her dad shook his head. "We don't want to tear the lining," he explained. "See how the hole is lined with strong plastic? That keeps the water from seeping into the ground."

"Real ponds don't have liners," Maddie said.

"No," Mom agreed. "But real ponds have springs or streams feeding into them, so whatever water seeps out is always being replaced."

Maddie grabbed a gobful of wet leaves — and shrieked. "It's a fish!" she said, horrified. "I found a dead goldfish!"

"Poor thing," Mom said. "It must have died over the winter."

"Somebody should have taken this fish inside when it got cold," Maddie said sternly.

"Actually," Dad said, "with the right care, goldfish don't need to come in for winter. Once we get this pond up and running, you'll see."

They kept cleaning.

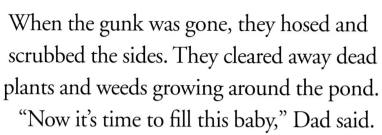

When the gunk was gone, they hosed and scrubbed the sides. They cleared away dead plants and weeds growing around the pond.

"Now it's time to fill this baby," Dad said. He put the hose in the middle of the pond. Maddie turned on the faucet full blast.

It took a long time to fill the pond. And then they had to turn on the pump — again. Only this time, instead of pumping water out, they were pumping air in.

"This keeps the water moving," Mom explained. "When water doesn't move around, it gets all stagnant and stinky. Fish and plants die. The springs and rivers feeding real ponds and lakes keep the water flowing. Our pond doesn't have any natural springs or streams. So we have to help."

Later that week they went to the plant store. They bought cattails and marsh marigolds, a long, slinky plant called eel grass, and water lilies.

"We have to have lilies," Dad said.

"They're kind of like shade umbrellas for the pond. They float on the water and keep the sun from making the water too hot.

And lilies help keep ponds clean. Their roots absorb nutrients so slimy pond scum can't grow."

Next they went to the fish store. "We need lots of goldfish!" Maddie told the woman behind the counter. "Big ones!"

The woman smiled. She took a little net and fished out three small goldfish.

"How about these?"

"But our pond is huge," Maddie protested.

"Well," said the woman, "fish grow — and they have baby fish. Last year I started with seven fish, and by the end of the summer I had over 200!"

Finally, they put everything in their pond. The plants bloomed, and the fish — Goldie, Spotty, and Sparkly — swam in and out of their green underwater jungle.

Butterflies landed on the lily pads, fanning their wings gently in the breeze. And one morning, Maddie found a frog sunning itself at the pond's edge!

"Hey," she said. "Where did you come from?"

Mom was trimming dead leaves from the pond plants. "Wherever there are ponds, there are frogs," she said. "Frogs know how to find water."

Maddie visited her pond every single day. But she was worried. "What are we going to do when it's winter?" she asked. "I don't want our fish to die, like that other one."

"They won't," Dad promised. "When it gets cold, we'll get a heater for the pond."

"Good," Maddie said. "Then Goldie and Spotty and Sparkly won't freeze."

"Well," said Dad, "they wouldn't freeze anyhow. They'd go down under the ice and swim really, really slowly at the bottom of the pond. When it's cold, goldfish don't even eat. They just wait for it to get warm again."

Maddie was confused. "Then why do we need a heater?"

"The heater will melt a hole in the ice. That way, fresh air can get into the water, and gases from rotting leaves and other dead stuff won't get trapped under the ice and poison the fish."

"Real ponds have a lot more cattails and reeds than we do." He broke off a cattail and showed it to Maddie. "See how it's hollow inside? Cattails and reeds act like straws. They poke through the ice and let bad gases out and good air in."

Maddie gazed into her pond. It was good to know that when winter came, her fish would be safe. While she drank hot cocoa and went sledding, Goldie and Spotty and Sparkly would be swimming slowly under the ice. And so would all the other baby fish that Maddie hadn't yet had time to name.

She liked everything about her new house — especially the pond she helped bring to life in the back garden!

Animal Eyes Underwater

Lobsters and crabs, including this hermit crab, have their eyes at the ends of long stalks. These animals can't move their heads, but their eyes can still peek around to look for food or predators.

Fish have to sleep with their eyes wide open. Why? Because they don't have eyelids. Eyelids help keep eyes from drying out.

What are the blue dots on the edge of a scallop's shell? Its eyes, of course. A scallop may not be able to see as clearly as you can, but it can detect the shadows of anything that swims near. And that's all a scallop needs to see to jet away or close up tight!

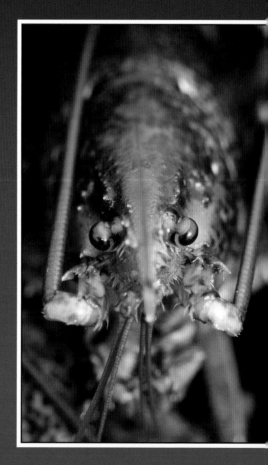

Glossary

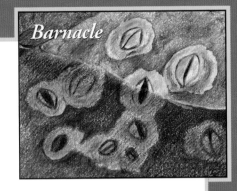
Barnacle

Algae: Tiny plants that live floating or suspended in water.

Ambush: To lie in wait to attack by surprise.

Artificial: Made by humans; not grown naturally.

Barnacle: A type of sea creature that in the adult stage of its life forms a hard shell and remains attached to a surface underwater, like a rock or ship bottom.

Buoyancy: Able to remain afloat in liquid or rise in air or gas.

Cell: The smallest part of an organism that is able to live by itself.

Crittercam: A small camera that can be attached to an animal and used to take photos wherever the animal goes.

Fertilize: To make something grow.

Migration

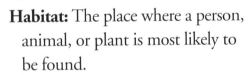
Habitat

Habitat: The place where a person, animal, or plant is most likely to be found.

Larva: The newly hatched, wingless, wormlike form of many insects before they become full grown.

Migration: Moving from place to place.

Neutral: Belonging to neither kind; not one thing or another.

Nutrient: A source of nourishment, or food that helps the body grow.

Predator: An animal that kills other animals for food.

Stagnant: Not moving or flowing; motionless.

Tentacle: A long armlike part of a squid, found around the mouth and used for feeling, grasping, or movement.

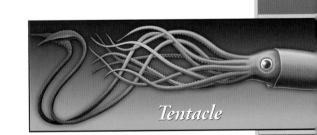
Tentacle

The World of WATER Animals

Aleutian
Islands

Alaska

California

North
America

United States

Atlantic

Ocean

South
America

Pacific

Ocean

N

W   E

S

Antarctica

Norway

Arctic Circle

Denmark

Europe

Asia

Africa

Indian

Ocean

Australia

Animals are Amazing!

All around the world, animals roam on the earth, in the sky, and under the water. Come explore the fascinating world of animals through a unique collection of stories inspired from the pages of *CLICK*® magazine. Travel with us as we meet many types of animals and discover all the amazing ways they enhance our world.

$17⁹⁵ each

Titles in the Animal Series

BUGS

PETS

WATER ANIMALS

WILD ANIMALS

Carus Publishing Company

Sea Star

Sea Star grips the rocky ocean bottom near shore. Waves crash over her, but she holds on tight. Tiny suckers underneath her five arms keep her in place. The suckers are on the tips of hundreds of little tubes that Sea Star uses as feet to crawl along the ocean floor.

The ocean waves carry the smell of clams to her. Sea Star is always ready for a meal. Her muscles pull water inside her body. Her tube feet fill like little balloons, and their suckers grab onto the sea floor. Then Sea Star squeezes the water out of some of her tube feet to pull herself forward. By pumping water in and out, Sea Star creeps closer and closer to the smell of clams.

When Sea Star reaches her goal, she climbs on top of a clam. The clam snaps its two shells closed, hiding its soft body. Clamping on with her tube feet, Sea Star tries to pry the shells open. She pulls and pulls, but the clam's strong muscles hold tight. Finally, Sea Star budges the shells apart.

Sea Star flips her stomach out through the mouth on her underside and into the tiny gap between the shells. She squirts chemicals that soften the clam's body. When the clam turns soupy, she swallows her meal. All that remains are two empty shells. After finishing her meal, Sea Star clings